Rising Stars 2017

**Organised by New Ashgate Gallery
in partnership with the University for the Creative Arts**

The competition is supported by the Billmeir Charitable Trust

New Ashgate Gallery
Waggon Yard
Farnham
Surrey GU9 7PS

newashgate.org.uk
Registered charity no. 274326

Editor and design: Camilla Dingee
Cover Image: Evgeniia Balashova, *Salmon and Cream Cheese Brooch*. Photographer: Evgeniia Balashova

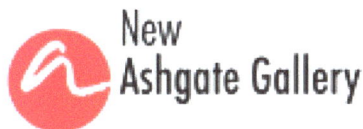
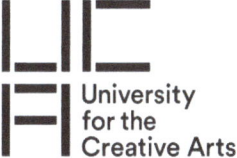

Celebrating the emerging talent

Rising Stars is a platform to view and collect some of the most exciting new craft by emerging makers from crafts and applied arts programmes across the UK. This curated exhibition is accompanied by professional development and a cash prize. In the past, many of the selected exhibitors have gone on to a high profile career and elite programmes such as Hothouse supported by the Crafts Council. Therefore, the exhibition is a great collector opportunity to learn more about the stars of the future.

The makers in the exhibition were selected following an open call for applications. We received more than 60 applications. The selection panel consisted of Rebecca Skeels, Post Graduate Subject & Senior Tutor for University of Creative Arts Farnham; Gemma Curtis, Craft Programme Co-ordinator, Farnham Maltings and Dr Outi Remes, Gallery Director, New Ashgate Gallery.

Opportunities such as *Rising Stars* are needed more than ever, as arts funding is being questioned and art organisations often focus on established artists that are less risky than presenting graduates or students.

The winner of the *Rising Stars* Award will be announced in the Rising Stars private view on 3rd March and she/he will receive a cash prize for professional development and a solo exhibition in the gallery. We hope that this will have a significant impact on the winner's career. The exhibition also has a related professional development programme that supports emerging creative talent – the participants of this exhibition and regional new talent.

Rising Stars is produced by New Ashgate Gallery in partnership with the University for the Creative Arts. It is supported by the Billmeir Charitable Trust. We would like to thank UCA and the Billmeir Charitable Trust for their continuing support for the project.

I hope that you enjoy the exhibition.

Dr Outi Remes
Gallery Director, New Ashgate Gallery Trust

Shortlisted artists and makers

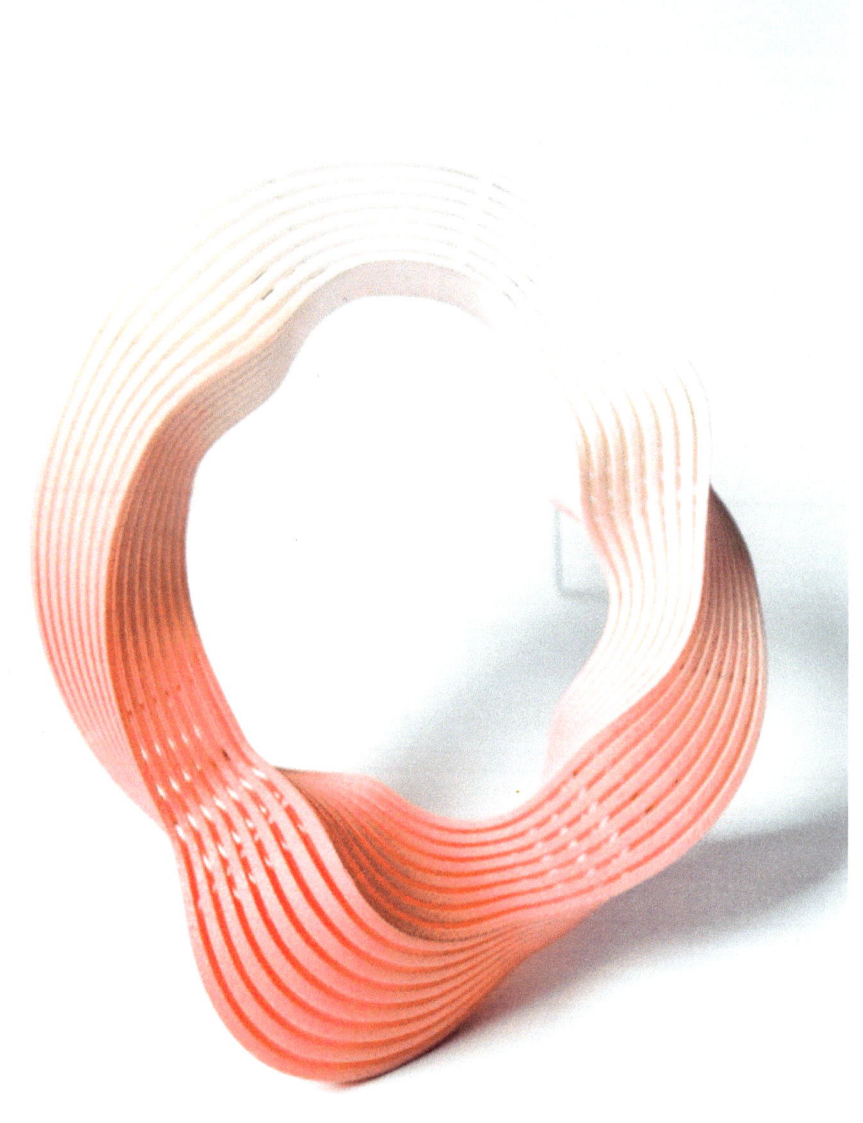

Evgeniia Balashova

2016 BA (Hons) Jewellery and Silversmithing, Glasgow School of Art

Evgeniia's work is inspired by the divergent nature of office spaces, and the objects of linear repetition which inhabit them: stationery, computer hardware and identical furniture. These objects are in perfect order, but once they experience human touch they turn into organized chaos. Evgeniia's work explores this curious relationship through a combination of contrasts. Through the use of digital technology and traditional hand skills she creates a balance between active and static, organic and geometric, machine and handmade. She uses the cube, a reference to an office cubicle, as a basis for many of her pieces. This acts as a starting point of transformation from a basic shape into a vibrant, energetic object.

She creates the pieces using a wide spectrum of making techniques. These include 3D printing, CNC milling, hand manufacturing, found objects, as well as direct recycling of IT hardware. Evgeniia aims to push the boundaries of material application by combining digital technology, heavy machinery and traditional hand skills.

Image: *Salmon and Cream Cheese Brooch*. Photographer: Evgeniia Balashova

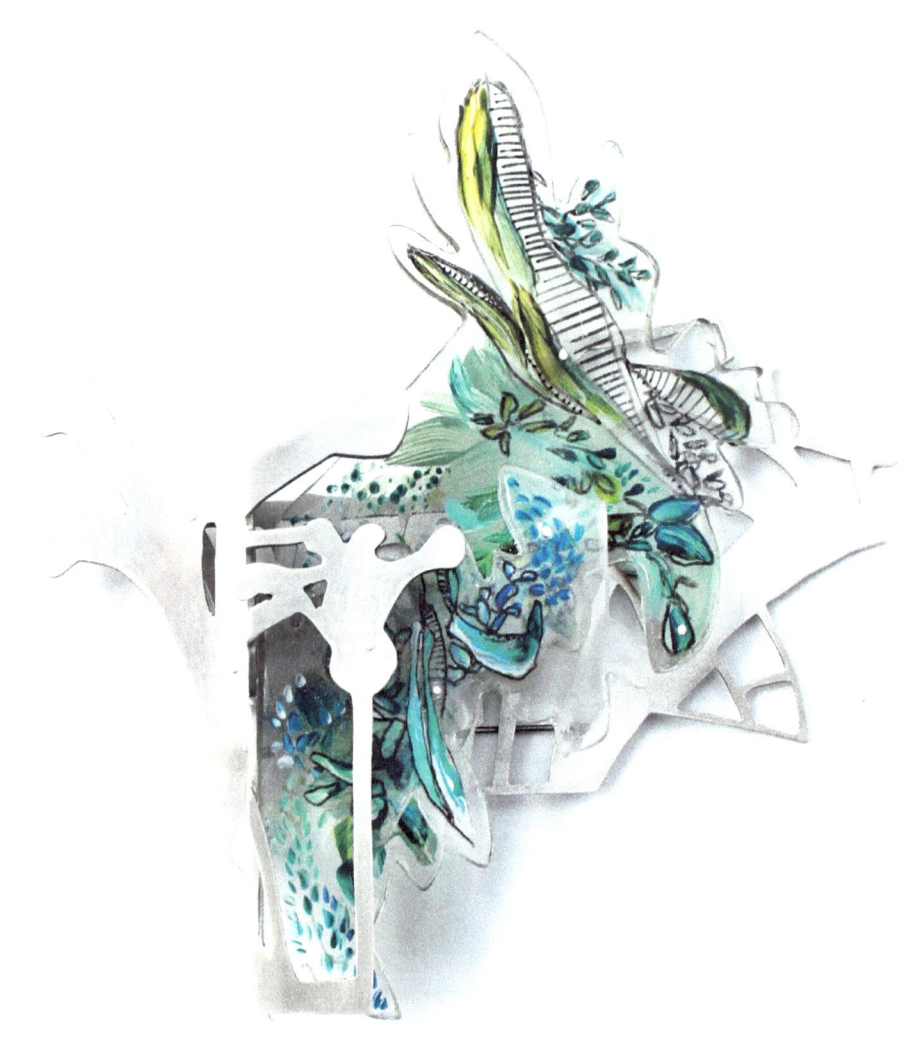

Holly Clifford

2016 BA (Hons) Jewellery Design & Related Products, Birmingham City University School of Jewellery

Holly describes herself as an Art Jeweller, crafting pieces of delicate and detailed wearable art that celebrates the curious attraction we have to plants and the natural world. Encompassing ideas from outside the realm of jewellery, her work draws from illustration, great painters such as Monet and Klimt, as well as from old dioramic books. Drawing and painting are an integral part of her creative process so she has developed ways to incorporate them into the jewellery itself.

Her work is inspired by both the beauty and chaos of gardens, being drawn to glasshouses and how these structures contrast against the abundance of botanical life trapped within. Holly focusses on scenes inside greenhouses, capturing the foggy nature of the glass and the foliage pressed up against the glass. She strives to capture the beauty of this combination using hand-painted scenes encased in resin, often combined with minimal metalwork or intricately pierced sheet. The translucent nature of the materials allows light to penetrate and play through the pieces; highlighting details within the paintwork and reflecting the layered, ephemeral elements of glasshouses. The methods used in the production of her work mean that each piece is a completely unique item of wearable art.

Image: *Victorian Glasshouse Brooch*, silver, resin, paint, steel. Photographer: Holly Clifford

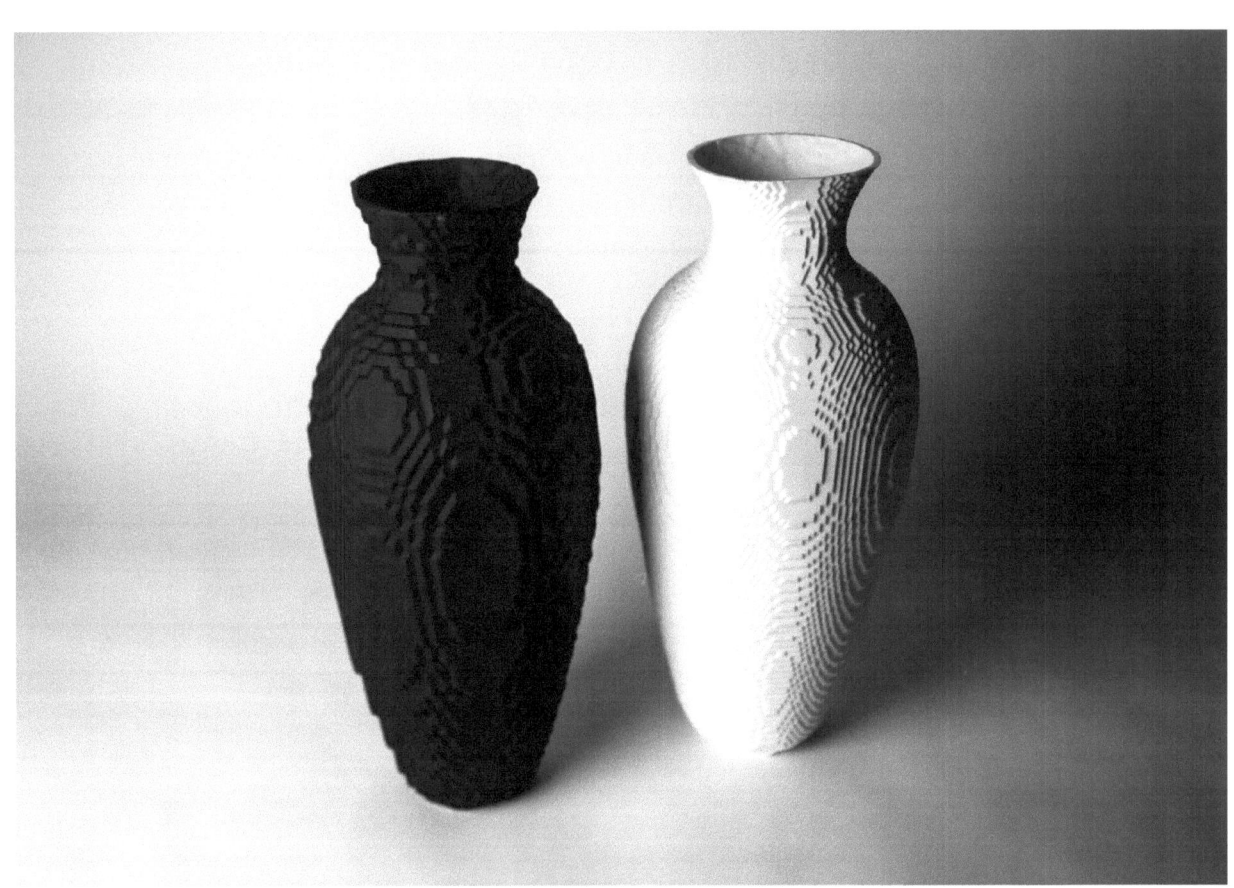

Matt Davis

2016 3D Design & Craft MDES, Brighton University

The boundaries between what is real and not real has become a difficult thing to discern in this postmodern age, and Matt's hyperreal vessels aim to address this development. His work attempts to bridge digital and analogue; working with computers and ceramics to challenge preconceptions of technology and traditional craft.

Digital techniques have been adapted in Matt's attempt to push the boundaries in what is possible with surface and form in ceramics. Multiple stages of software are used to generate models that are 3D printed, moulded and slip cast in bone china & black porcelain. The resulting physical pixels are hyper realistic objects which appear to be virtual in the physical world.

Aiming to explore the manifestation of digital objects in physical space; this theme of duality relates to the processing of intangible code, the decomposing nature of organic clay and the transformation from temporal data into immortalised ceramics.

Image: *Hi-res & Lo-res Vessels*, bone china and porcelain. Photographer: Matt Davis

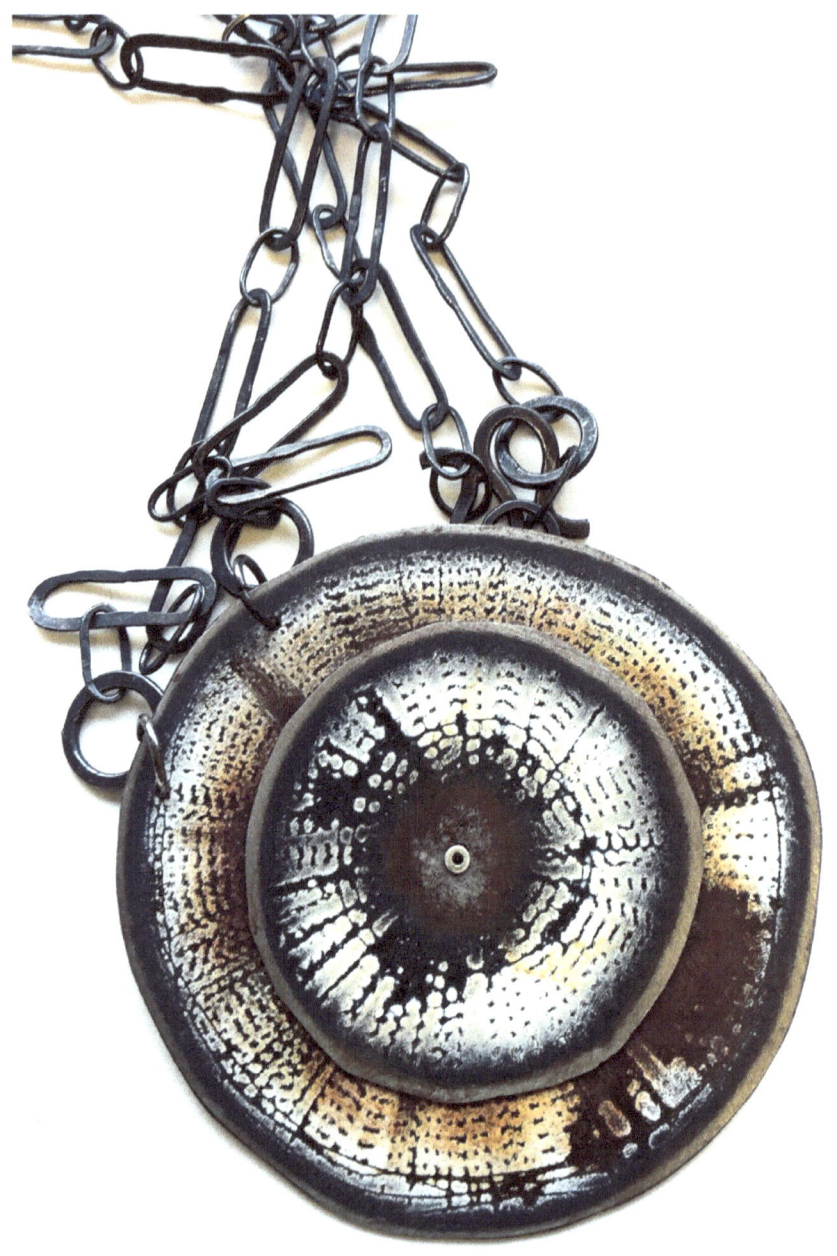

Amanda Denison

2014 BTEC Level 3 Jewellery, Kingston and Chelsea College

2014 Professional Practice, Kensington & Chelsea College

Amanda has lived in London all her life and is inspired by the traces left behind through decay, dilapidation and the textures and marks stamped on the urban environment. She is drawn to repeated elements that distort and change while her fascination with pattern and surface textures translates into her pieces. Her fine art background influences her approach; she draws into the enameled surfaces which becomes a means with which to explore and develop mark making.

She works with precious and non-precious metals and enjoys the challenge of combining industrial materials (steel and wet process enamel) with traditional processes to create distinctive textural pieces. She incorporates patinas and enamels to add colour, although her palette is subtle and restrained. While most makers build up highly coloured layers of enamels, she restricts hers to one or two. Amanda deconstructs the enamelled surfaces removing the glassy surface to create a smooth matt exterior with subtle areas of hue and tone. When patches of bare steel are revealed they are encouraged to rust. The end result is a richly degraded enamel surface and a unique piece of contemporary art jewellery. Despite repeating this process, there is always an element of chance and no two pieces are ever exactly the same.

Image: *Traces neckpiece,* enamelled steel, rusted with oxidised silver chain. Photographer: Amanda Dension

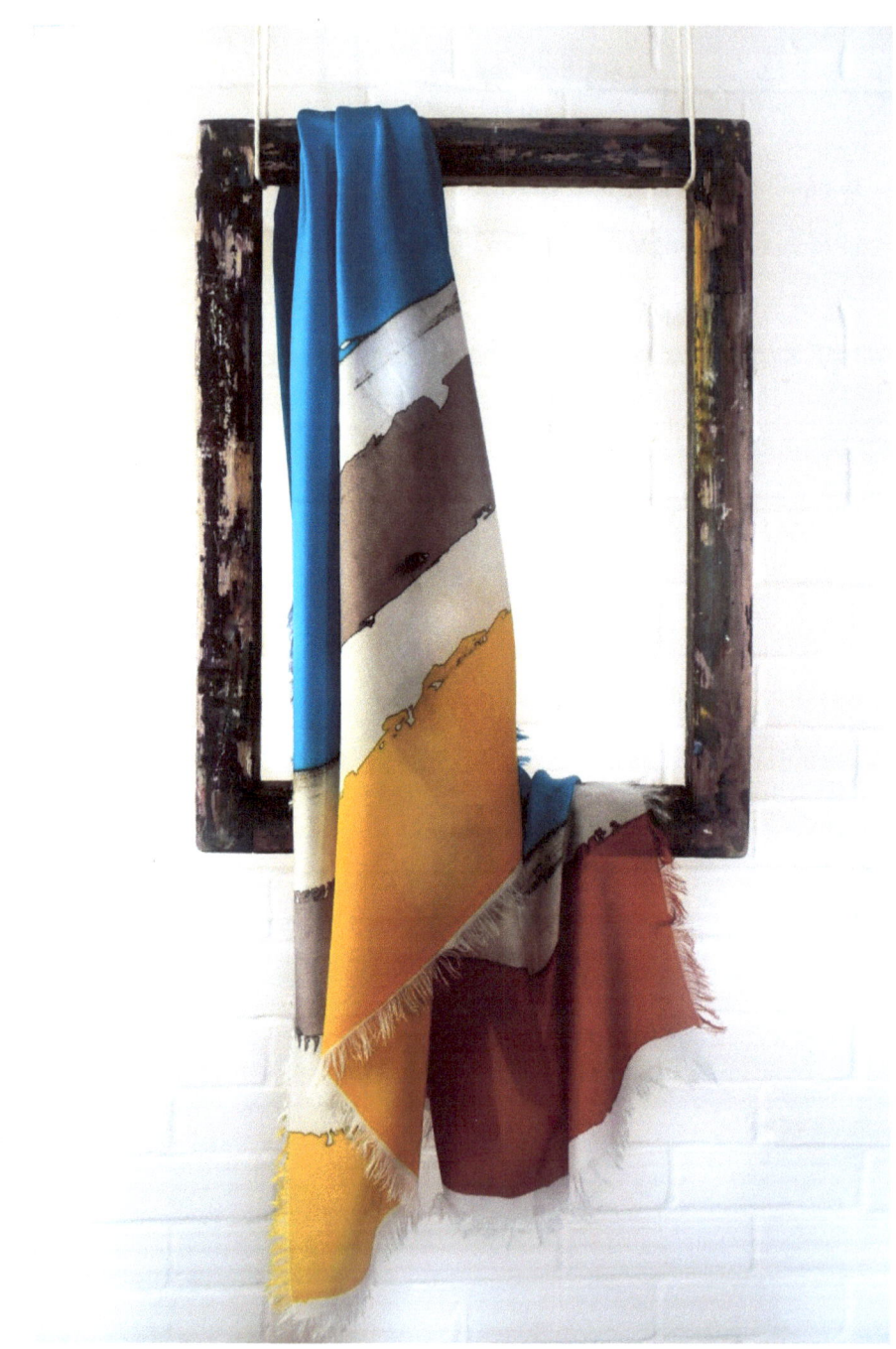

Joanna Hayward

2014 BA (Hons) Textiles for Fashion or Interiors, UCA, Farnham

For Joanna, screen printing is not just about transferring an image onto a material. It's about the relationship with the sequence of the process; the physical measuring of colour and chemicals, experimentation with pastes, the pushing and pulling through a screen and the finishing processes. Joanna enjoys these exciting hands on methods of printing and the end result is a bonus. Her work embraces colour and how it can come alive through shape and scale, especially on cloth. Shapes and colour can be as free as you want them to be, and she makes the most of playful, contemporary design.

The pieces created can be unexpected, original and solitary, as Joanna tends to use a breakdown printing method which cannot allow her to produce any two pieces alike. She uses this method regularly in her prints as the outcome can relate very clearly to her inspiration of deteriorating surfaces such as peeling paint or corroding metal. Joanna enjoys creating raw edges through energetic mark making to deliver an expressive conversation between colour and shape - mainly using milk fibre and silk georgette textile base as their qualities allow the colours and shapes to become rich and elegant.

Image: *No. M1,* screen print on milk fibre, procion dye pastes. Photographer: Joanna Hayward

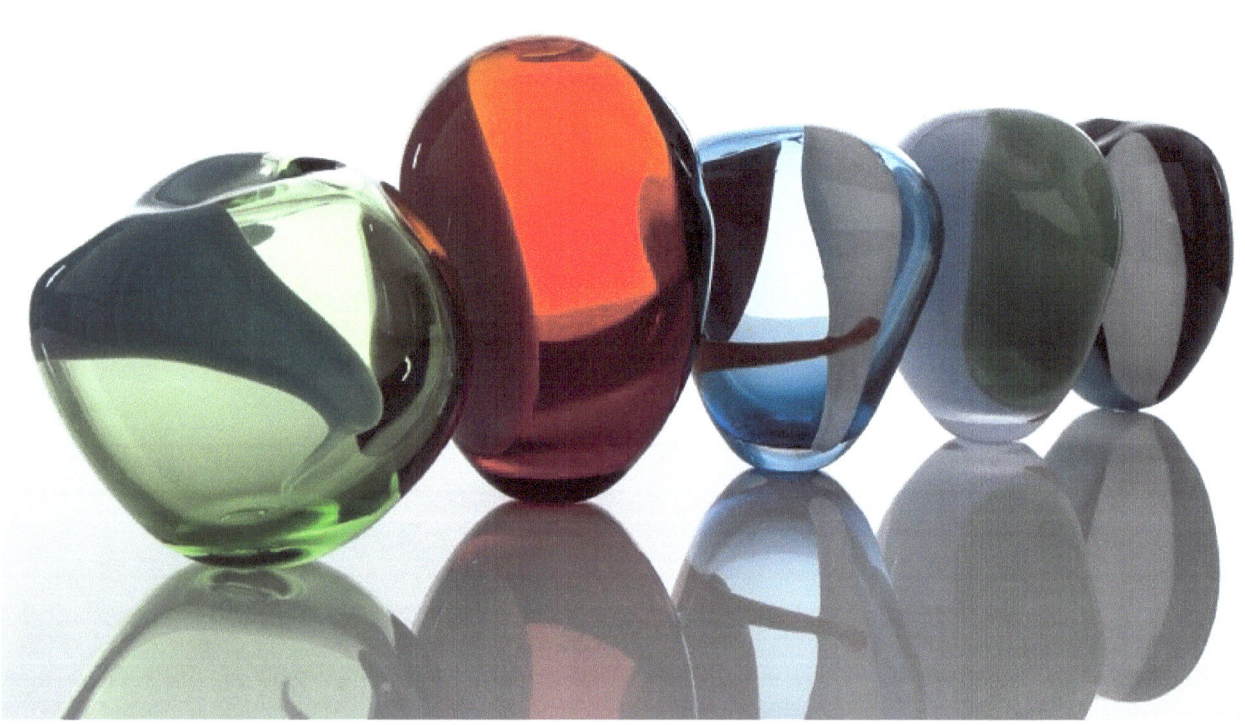

Alice Heaton

2016 BA (Hons) Design Craft, De Montfort University

Alice is a Cheshire based designer who specialises in working with hot glass. Taking inspiration from nature she produces richly colourful and dynamic individual blown sculptural pieces. Her current collection *Life Within* focuses on the bold intensely coloured microscopic creatures, sponges and coral that exist in our oceans. She works with the glass, applying vivid colour combinations based on those found underwater, until it is almost at the point of collapse. Capturing the dynamic movement caused by the force of sub aqua currents, the pieces she creates are expressive and uninhibited sculptural objects.

Alice is currently Artist in Residence in the Art and Design Faculty at De Montfort University, developing her *Life Within* collection further by exploring in more detail the use of her colour palette. She is also using the opportunity to explore other ideas, based on the natural world including wood and forest treelines, and making processes, so that both her design and practical skills base are pushed in to new areas.

Image: *Life Within*, blown glass. Photographer: Nigel Essex

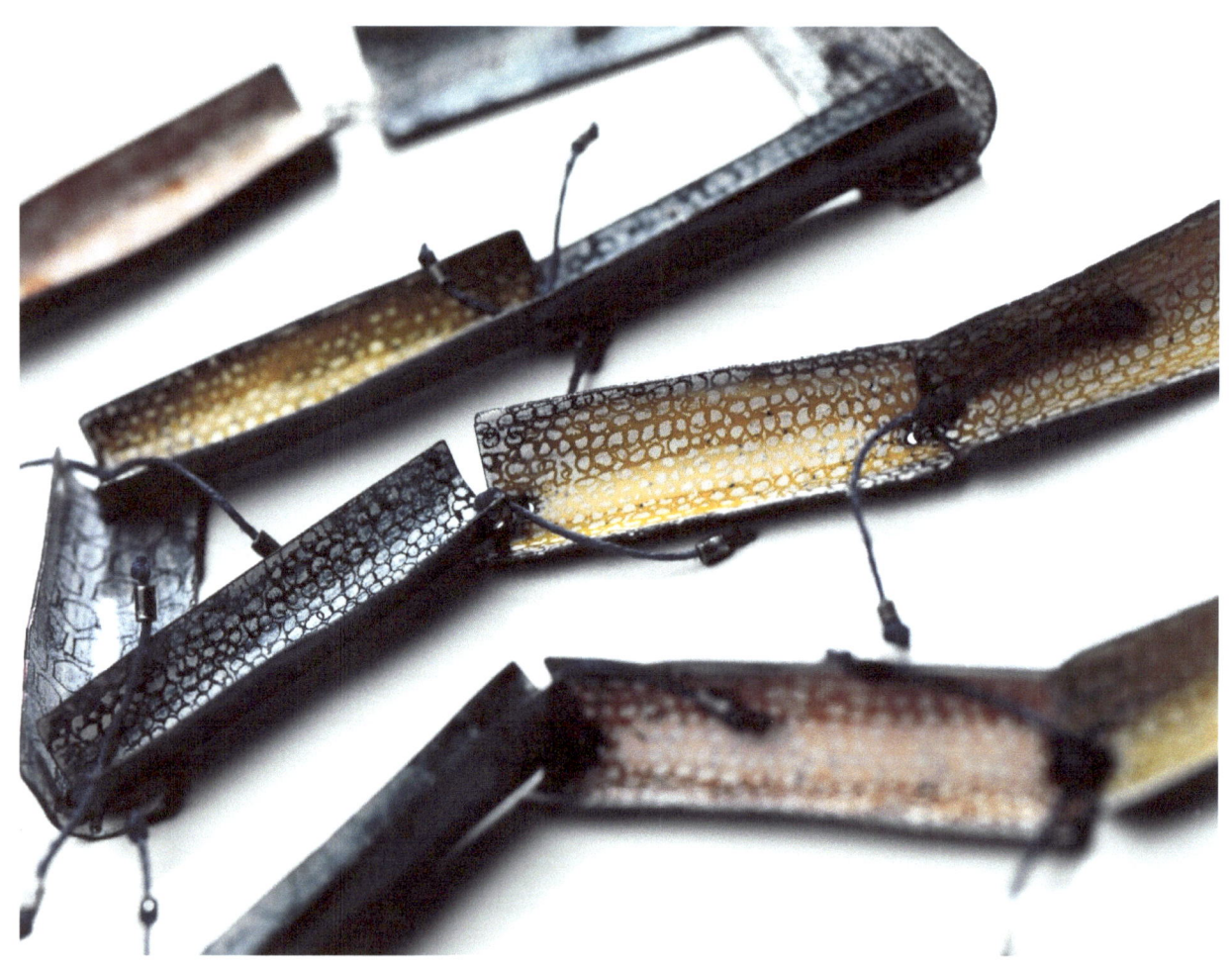

Emily Higham

2016 BA Hons Jewellery and Silversmithing, Edinburgh College of Art

Beehives and the beautiful gradient colours of honey and honeycomb inspired Emily's current jewellery collection. Her jewellery aims to portray the beautiful colours and the aesthetical, fragile and organic quality beehives and honeycomb hold, whilst still holding resemblance of the structural shapes found within hives.

Emily took inspiration from the rectangular shapes of beehive boxes and the layers they are built upon; stacked in a neat uniform line above each other, contrasted with the organic unpredictability of how the honeycomb itself grows and forms around the frames within the hive boxes. These layers are then translated into formed metal and enamel, resembling the layers built up within beehive boxes, both within the outside of the box and the rectangular slots hidden inside. This process of enamelling allows Emily to build up gradient layers of colours, marks and surface patterns which are then removed, scratched back and stacked up to reveal a collection of unpredictable marks and varied assortments of colour. The drawing process is also a major influence that has informed Emily's collection. Her inspiration lies heavily within a sketchbook, taking influences from the qualities within printmaking and the combined collections of colours through college. Her drawings are then translated into the versatile and aesthetic medium of enamel, which acts as a type of unpredictable drawing.

Image: *Tied Enamel Necklace*, enamel, copper, silver and linen thread. Photographer: Shannon Tofts

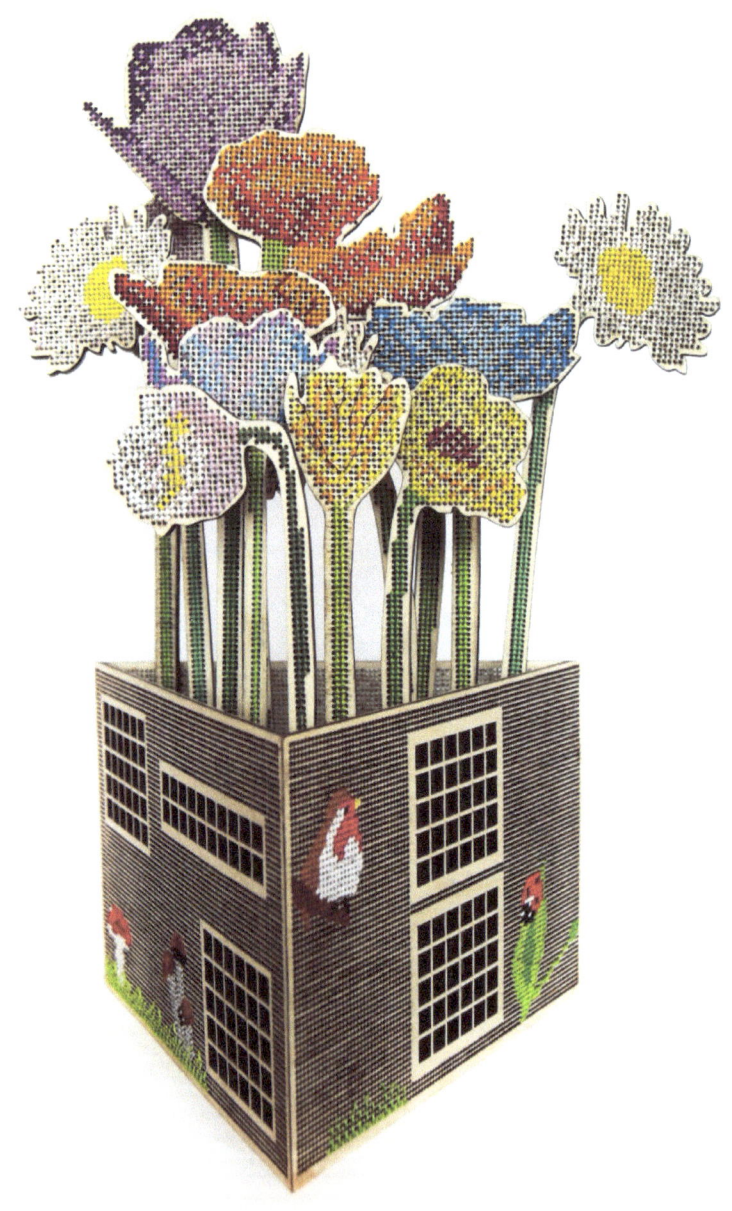

Isabel Howe

2015 BA (Hons) Contemporary Craft, Falmouth University

Contemporary crafts maker Isabel is inspired by her love of nature and fairy tales. She specialises in laser cut embroidery, a technique she has developed using a laser cutter, wood, and silk threads to create her unique work. This technique is something she has developed over the years, using flowers as an inspiration in a new and intriguing way. She enjoys the mix of contemporary techniques with traditional elements. Her work is a modern take on the Berlin Wool Work technique, traditionally used on tapestries. Using flowers, Isabel explores their Victorian Floriography meanings to create a sense of wonder encouraging a closer look at the details, which broadens the imagination.

She enjoys incorporating different cultures and countries into her designs, some of her upcoming work is inspired by Rome and London. Isabel is currently expanding her ranges, working on some larger scale pieces and experimenting to combine embroidery and painting.

Image: *Flower House*, plywood, and silk threads. Photographer: Emily Hardwick

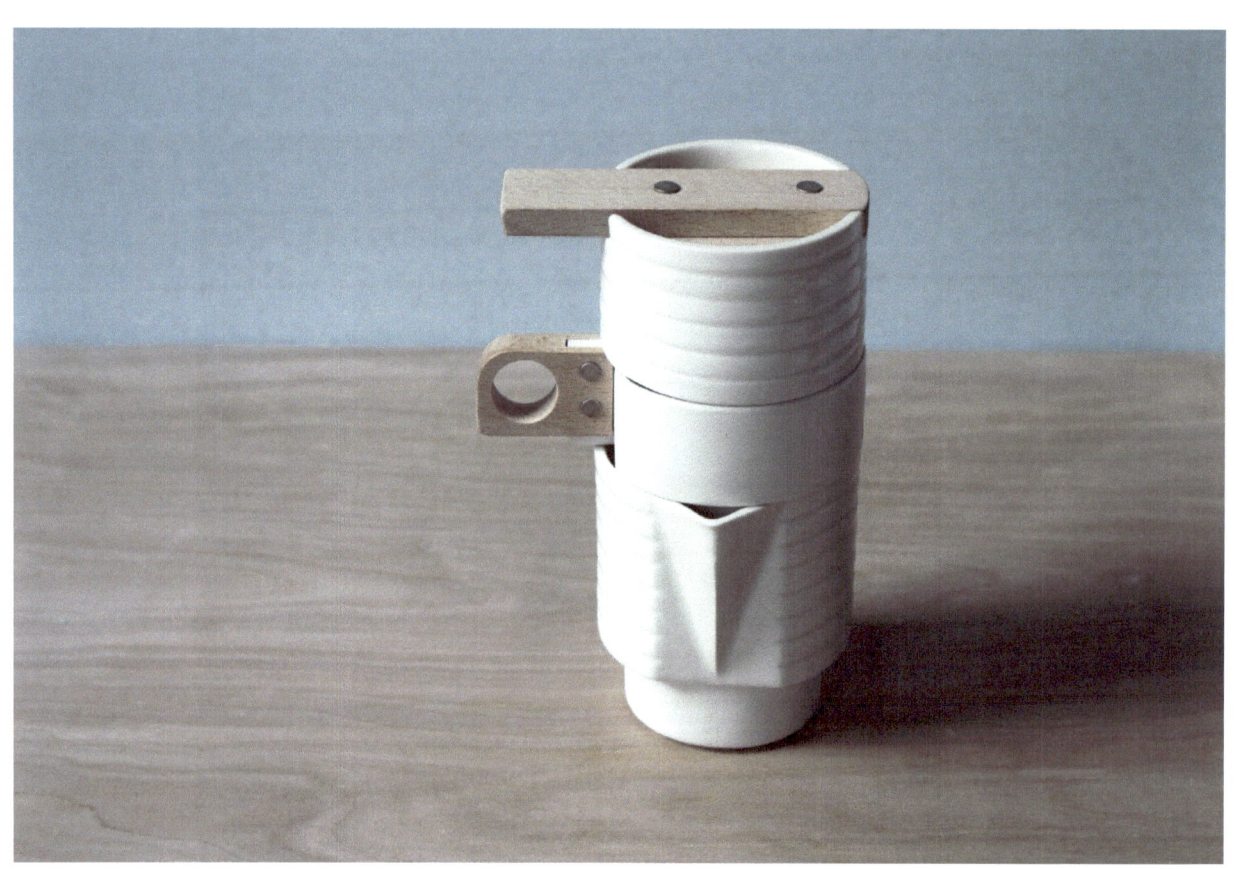

Emma Johnson

2016 MDes 3D Design and Craft, University of Brighton

Emma specialises in mould made ceramics. Her work is often inspired by architectural details; incorporating precise and angular forms along with a degree of buildability and a unified combination of materials.

Emma's latest collection *Atro-City* explores the revival of Brutalist architecture. At its time of emergence in post-war Britain, Brutalist architecture intended to symbolise a modern utopia. It aimed to provide a new type of social housing which would transform society through architecture, but by the 1970s it had gained a negative reputation; being labelled as ugly, inhuman and brutal. Recently, however, people have begun to embrace these post-war 'concrete monstrosities' and the popularity of buildings including the Barbican and Trellick Tower has increased dramatically.

The functional objects, which revolve around the serving of tea, incorporate typical Brutalist aesthetics such as heavy forms and asymmetrical proportions. Brutalist design philosophies including Form Follows Function, Truth to Materials and Synthesis of Hand and Machine are also explored, with carefully considered design choices reflecting these notions. Instead of using typical aesthetics associated with concrete, the collection aims to show the shift in opinion surrounding Brutalism, portraying it in a fresh and modern light far away from past brutal associations.

Image: *Atro-City Stacked*, porcelain, stoneware glaze, beech components, nickel silver rivets. Photographer: Emma Johnson

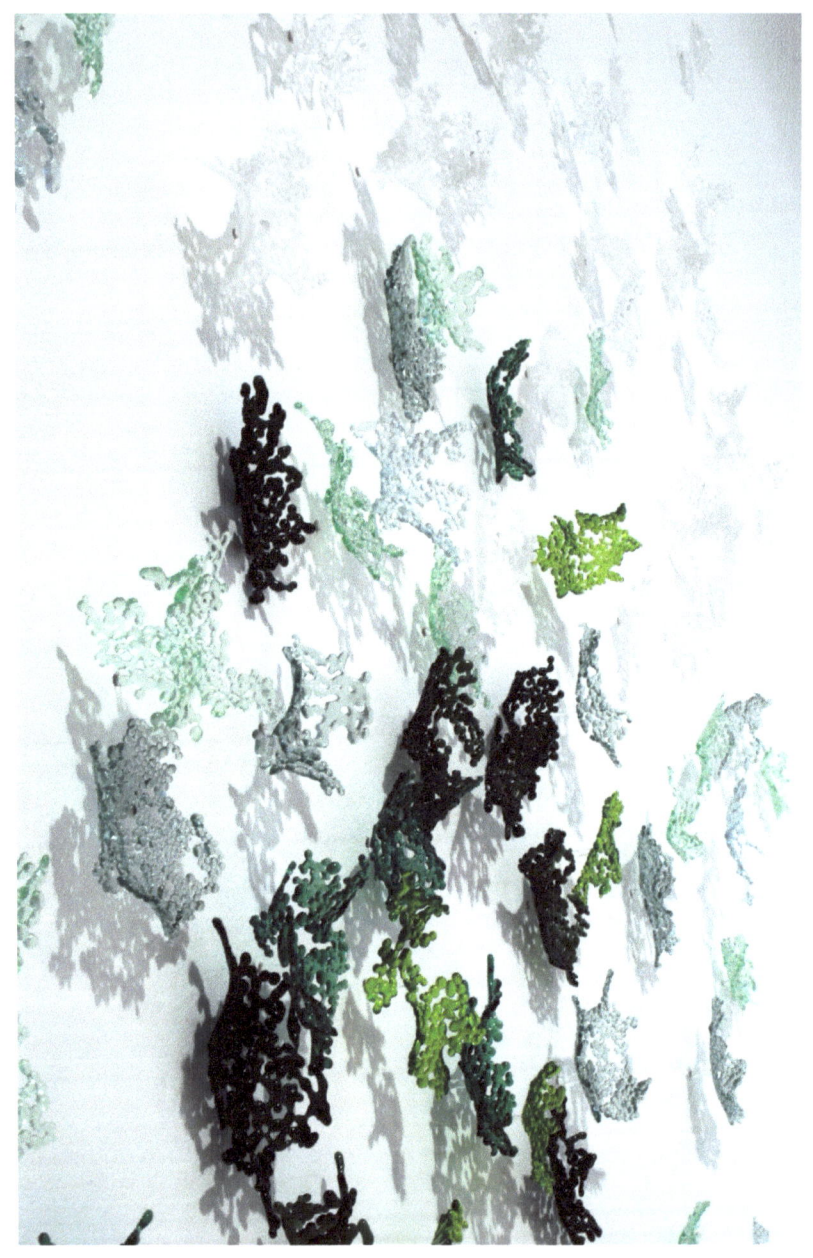

Monette Larsen

2014 MA Royal College of Art, London

2008 Glass Art degree, Royal Danish Academy of Fine Arts, Bornholm, Denmark

Starting from the idea that what we perceive as beautiful in nature is linked to the conscious or unconscious recognition of underlying patterns and structures, Monette looks at molecular structures, nanoscale and mathematics in the natural world as a foundation for her work. With these influences she creates forms, which suggest movement and life that reference and hint at the natural world without mimicking it. The aim is to remind the viewer of the beautiful living world around us.

Transformed Nature aims to remind us of what natural forms can offer us, opening our eyes to what is around us. The complex glass framework is inspired by the underlying structure of corals, increasingly fragile as a result of the degradation of oceans caused by humans, and rising temperatures from global warming. The installation consists of unique pieces made up of small glass spheres arranged into formations, fused together and slumped into shapes.

Monette spent a year developing her craft as an Artist in Residence at the University of Creative Arts, Farnham. Her glasswork is designed for interior spaces where the glass can play with light and the shadows can add depth to the delicate pieces.

Image: *Aspiring Nature,* fused and slumped glass. Photographer: Monette Larsen

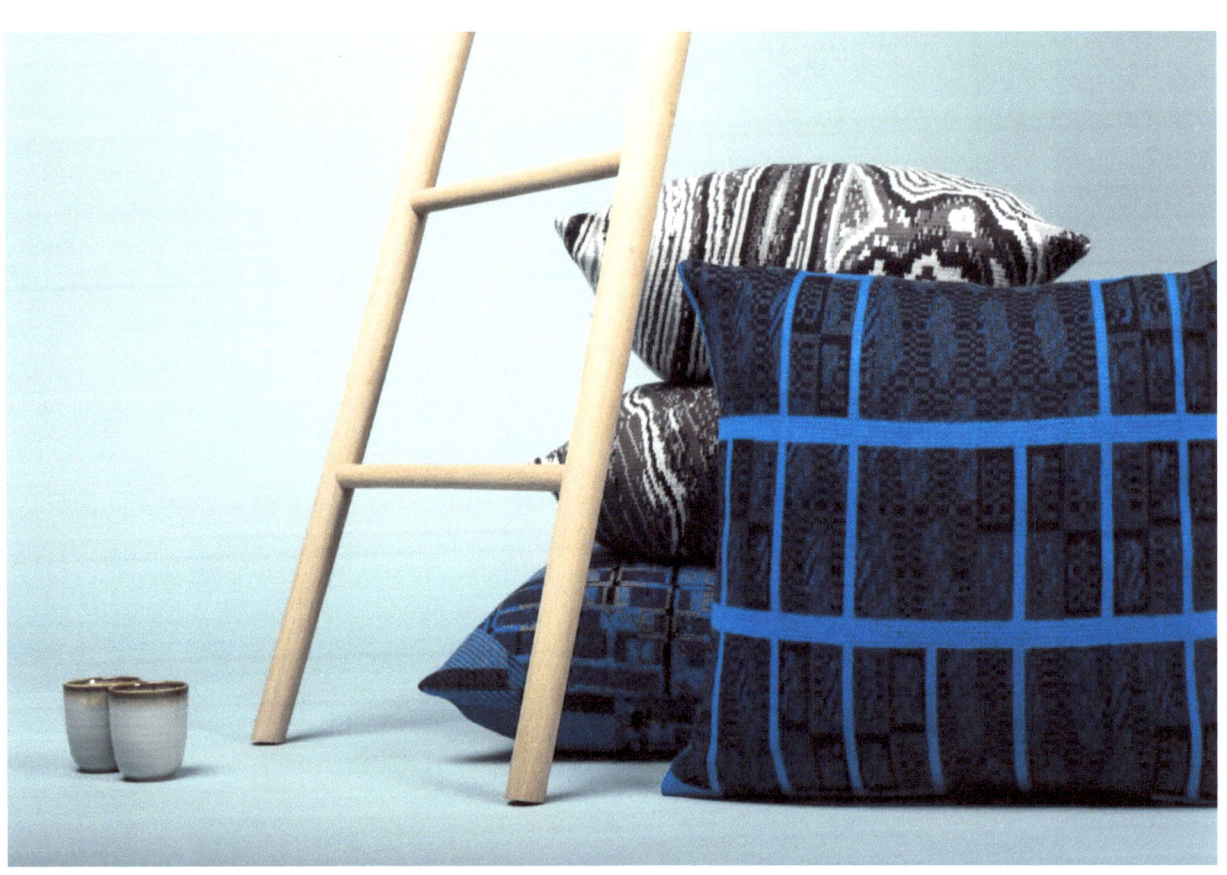

Danny Lee

2014 MA Textiles, Royal College of Art, London

2012 BA (Hons) Art Practice, Goldsmiths, University of London

Danny is a fabric developer and textile artist based in London. He uses innovative craft techniques, the latest machinery, and Italian yarns of the highest quality to produce beautiful and functional textile pieces that can inspire and compliment the home. Danny Lee Designs aims to enrich everyday living experience with high quality, artisan creativity and useable art.

In the collection, the runners and blankets are made of 100% Merino wool and the cushions are just the right fusion of Merino wool and Peruvian cotton. This season, Danny has also worked with selected UK factories, using the latest knitwear technology to produce his highly technical and hand worked textile homeware.

The Spring/Summer 2017 collection uses graphic collages, drawing inspiration from constructing skyscrapers imbedded with his signature weave structure motifs.

Image: *Grid Cushion Blues Colour way,* Merino wool and Peruvian cotton, Photographer: Robin Sinha

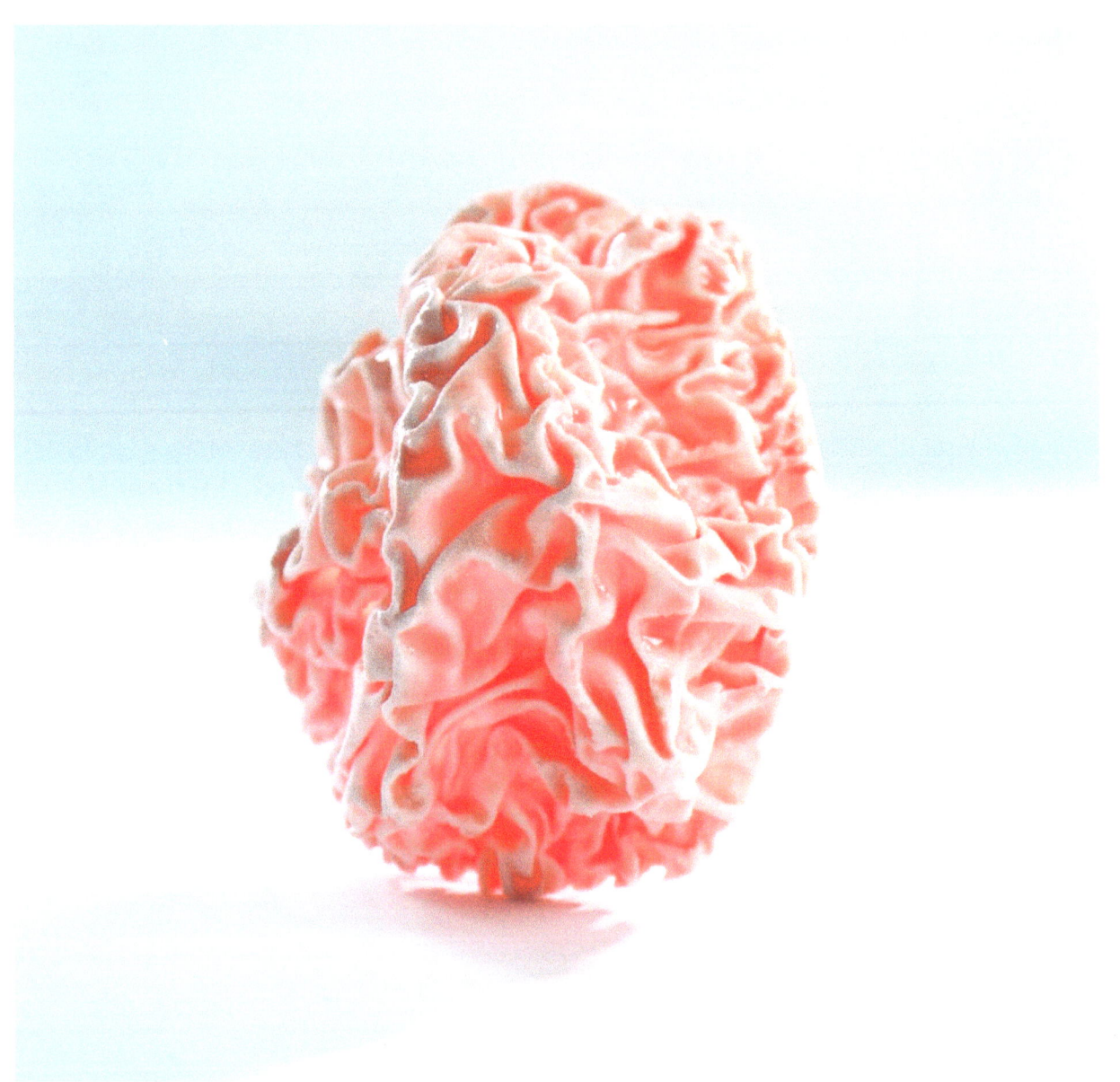

Karen Lester

2016 MA Contemporary Jewellery, Silversmithing and Related Products, Birmingham School of Jewellery

2013 BA (Hons) Design Craft, De Montfort University

The fragility of impermanence is the notion that has informed Karen's work. Each piece represents the fluidity of life and how relentless but subtle pressure is embedding its mark. Her work embraces both process and material, and consists of a multi layered approach. Using a combination of textile and ceramic techniques, a skin is formed and then manipulated. Through external pressure and destruction a new aesthetic emerges, traces of the original skin entwined with the new.

Traditionally held concepts about the material, bone china, allows Karen to exploit ideas of fragility and strength. The final outcome is dictated by heat from the kiln, resulting in each piece being a unique and individual wearable sculpture.

Image: *Fluidity Series II Brooch*, Bone China, Glaze, Silver, Photographer: Karen Lester

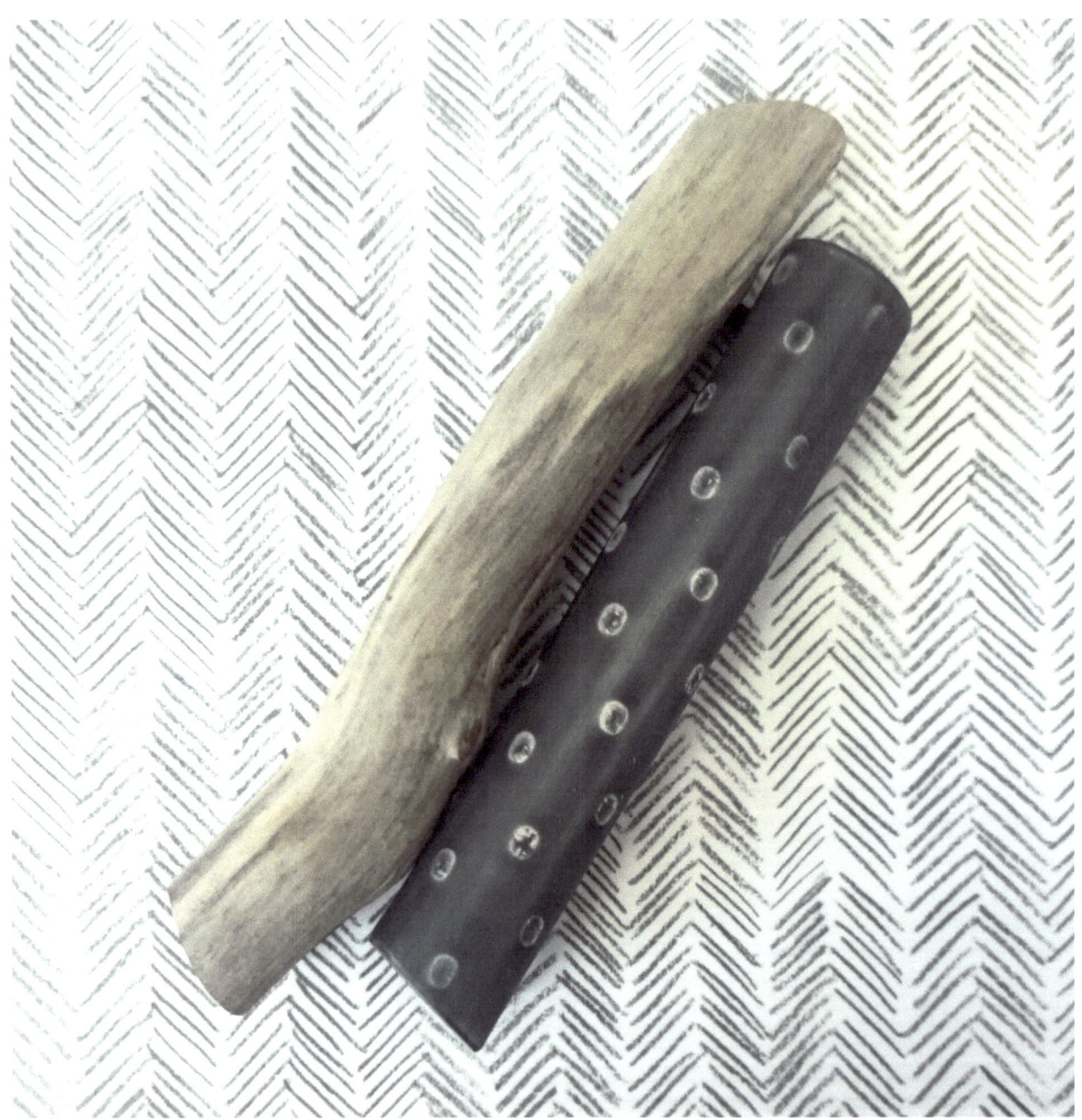

Tina MacLeod

2015 BA (Hons) Silversmithing and Jewellery Design, The Glasgow School of Art

Tina is a Scottish designer/maker who returned to the West Highlands in 2015 to set up her studio after graduating. She creates tactile pieces of jewellery that evoke a sense of place. The concept of the island and the unique atmosphere of the Hebridean coastal woodland are central to her work, capturing an essence of that sensed but unexplained aura often experienced within the forest. By using precious metal techniques that produce delicate but deliberate layers of surface texture, she is able to convey a sense of the ephemeral nature of the living landscape.

Designing through making, Tina works intuitively with natural materials gathered from specific places, and by exploring hollow forms, creating jewellery which represents a connection to place which is realised through the importance of touch. Ultimately, each object becomes a representation of the viewer and wearer's story, the original meaning transcends. The origin belongs to the maker, embedded within the piece but the meaning distorts and evolves as different people find their own connection with it.

Image: *Lorg series Brooch*, silver, wood. Photographer: Tina MacLeod

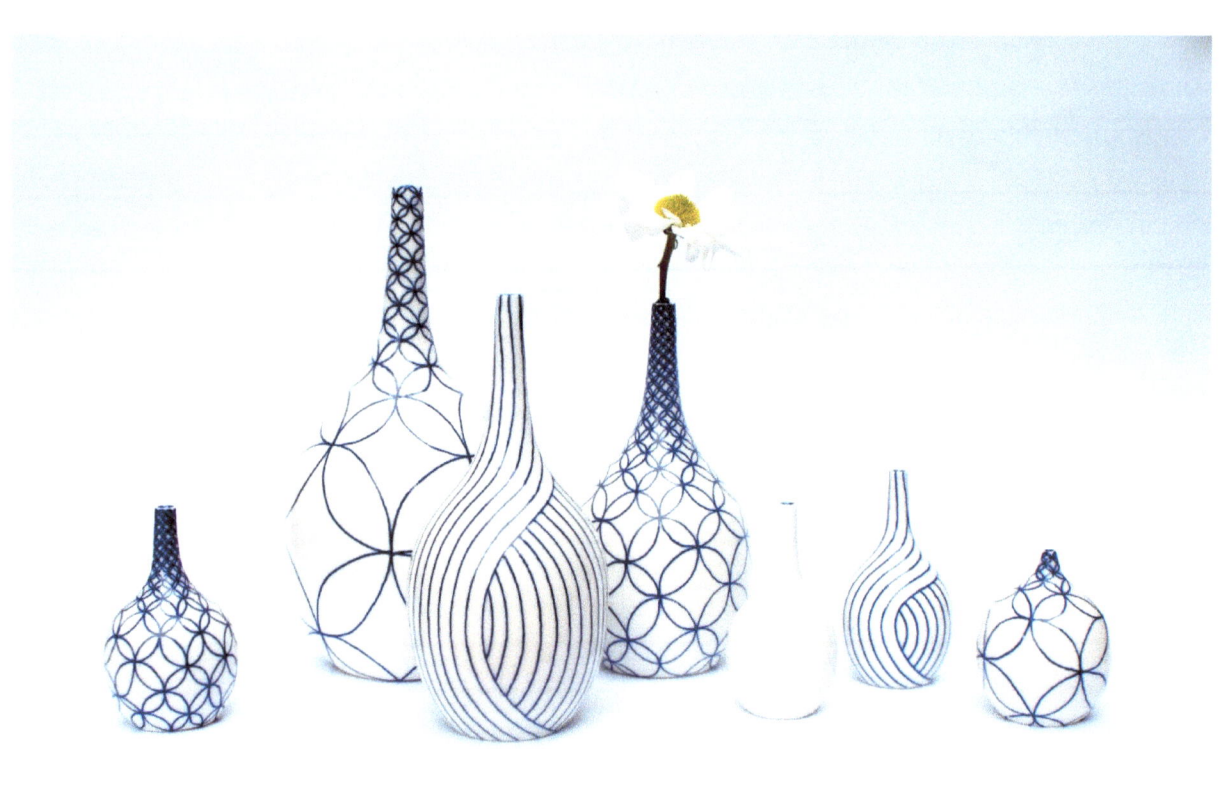

Rhian Malin

2014: BA (Hons) Three Dimensional Design, Camberwell College of Art

Rhian is an artist based in Stratford upon Avon, Warwickshire. Inspired by her Grandmother's Willow Pattern collection, Rhian continues the long historic tradition of hand-painting porcelain with cobalt-blue decoration. Her elegant wheel-thrown porcelain vessels are the chosen surface to stretch this tradition into the 21st Century.

The beauty of imperfection is explored through applying geometric patterns to deliberately distorted forms, challenging the inherent perfectionist Rhian is at heart. Taking a mathematical approach to applying each design, patterns are either projected onto vessels to accentuate their tactile, dimpled contours or divided up into eighths vertically to highlight their tapering forms.

Image: *Contour Bottles,* thrown porcelain with hand-painted patterns. Photographer: Rhian Malin

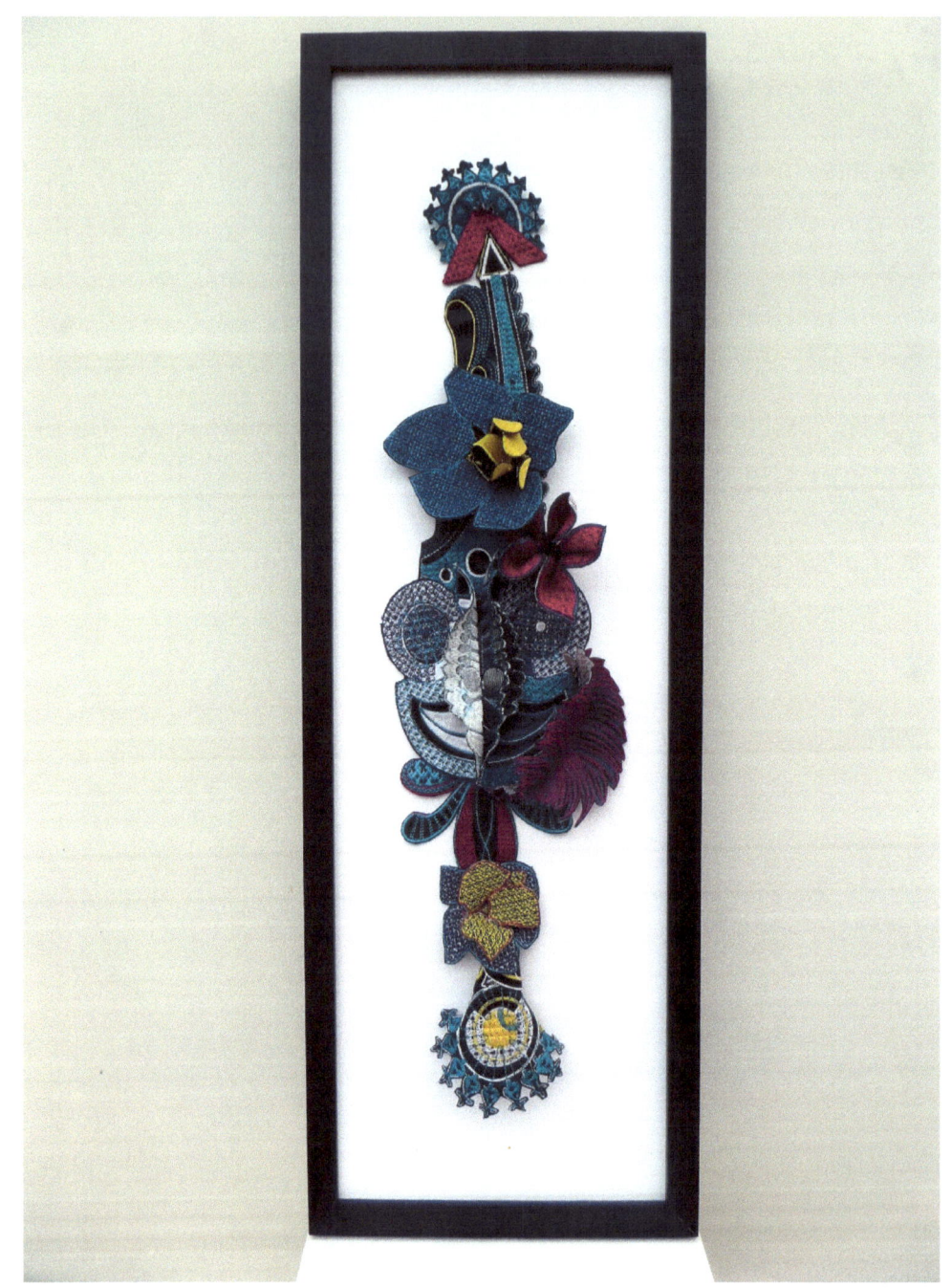

32

Laura Marriott

Ba (Hons) Textile Design, Birmingham City University

Laura is a embroidery artist based in Derby with a passion for digital stitch creating colourful, illustrative designs. She loves pushing the boundaries of digital embroidery by stretching and layering stitches to create unusual and exciting textures. With multiple techniques, Laura's work investigates exciting ways of how embroidery can be formed into fabric itself, creating innovative lace forms that are bold and unique. Her current project *Digital Tribe* is inspired by a deep cultural fascination with tribal art and traditional objects accumulated on personal travels. Each shape is designed separately, then carefully selected to form 3D, hand manipulated, playful motifs.

Laura was awarded Graduate of the Year 2016 by The Textile Study Group; and a stand at the Knitting and Stitching Shows in London and Harrogate by The Embroiderer's Guild. These opportunities helped Laura launch her studio, which led to her getting accepted into the Design Factory in December 2016.

Image: *DublinTotem*, digital embroidery. Photographer: Laura Marriott

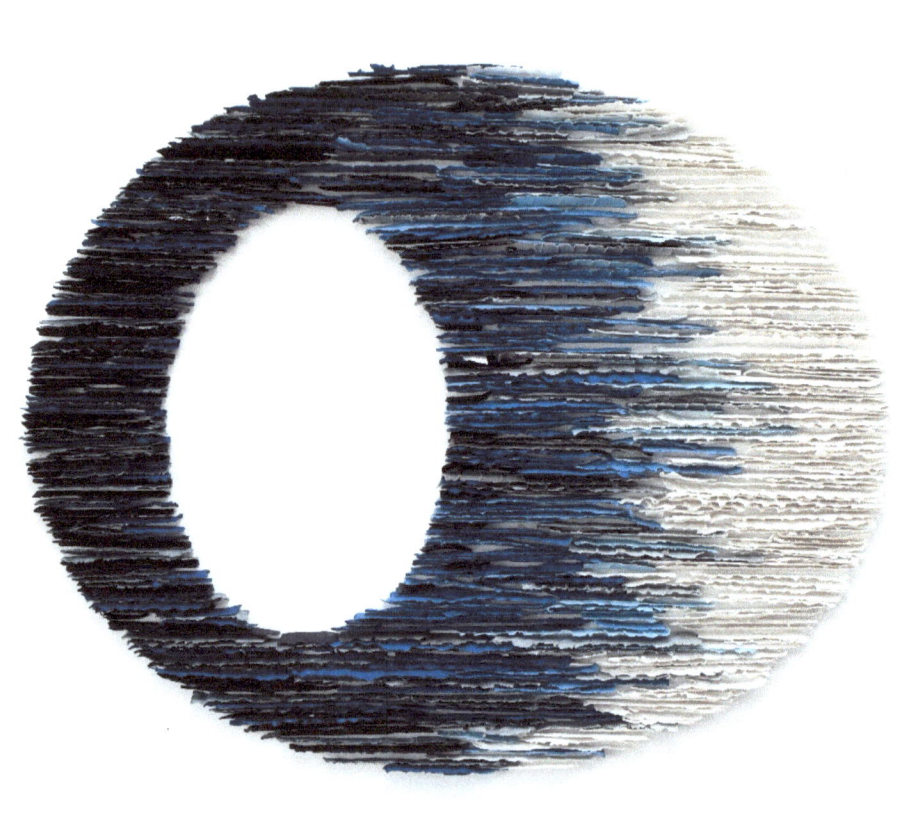

Julie Massie

2016 MA Ceramics UCA, Farnham

1989 BA (Hons) Christ Church College Canterbury

Julie's art work is inspired by looking and seeing what is around her own environment by the Dorset coast. Her ideas are drawn from direct observation: recorded by photography, drawing or impression and images from memory. She takes inspiration from the simplest things and adapts them to make ceramic wall art.

The Jurassic Coastline has been a constant source of inspiration, engaging with the fragility of the beautiful, interesting and internationally important landscape. Coasts are a product of erosion and without the sea eroding the land we would not have a coastline. The main threat to the continuation of these natural processes is the construction of coastal defenses such as sea walls, rock armour and gabions. These engineering structures disrupt the natural coastal processes of erosion and attempt to stabilise the cliffs, promoting vegetation growth which then obscures the geology and fossils. The fragile edges of her work represent the beauty and importance of this eroding landscape by the sea. Julie has also taken inspiration from the edges of waves breaking onto the shore and the different strength of these waves constantly breaking onto the shoreline. These strong and destructive waves are the primary shapers of the coastline and usually occur in the winter when the sea is cold and grey, intermingled with blues. These colours and the fragility of this coast are both reflected within her final outcomes while also exploring the senses, especially touch, sight and sound.

Image: *Oval Edges*, porcelain. Photographer: Jay Simpson

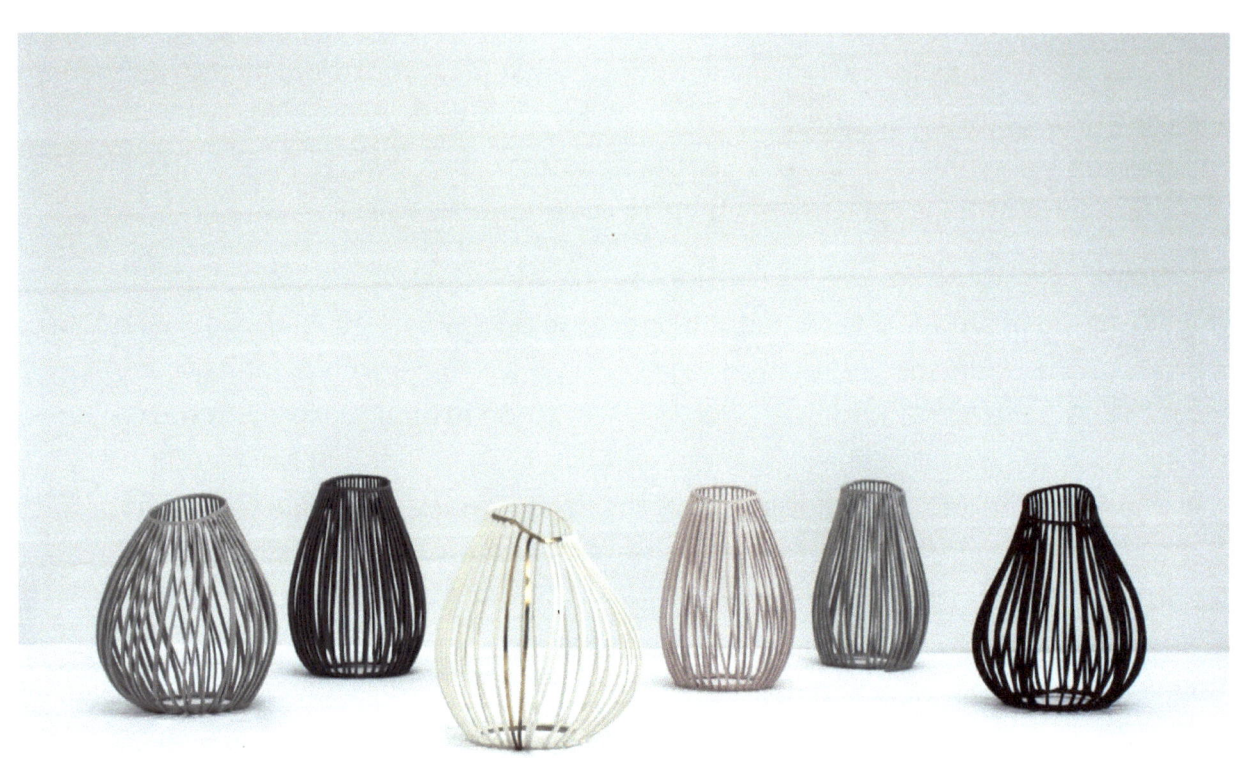

Lauren Nauman

2016 MA Ceramics & Glass, Royal College of Art, London

2012 BA Art Education, Emmanuel College, Boston, MA, USA

Lauren's work explores the boundaries within clay through experimental processes. She starts with the industrial method of plaster moulds and slip-casting; however, she doesn't always use these in traditional ways. With her current project *Lines*, she uses metal as an aesthetic reference and material contrast. An additive method is used to create pieces with minimal amounts of clay. This body of work has become an engaging display of how clay moves in the kiln. The suggestions of vessels start out as straight cages of wet clay and through the power of the kilns heat and the pyro-plasticity of the clay, they move like fabric to evolve into a wire-like sculpture that still hold the materiality of porcelain. Due to this process, the final form of each piece stems from minute details in the making, but mostly depends on chance.

"The Line of Beauty: Lauren Nauman is a ceramicist with an experimental bent. Her *Lines* series of vases, jars and dishes uses porcelain and brass in thin strips to create vessels which look rigid and fragile at the same time. The shapes are also intriguing: some look controlled and precise, others delightfully random; a beautiful exercise in contradictions."[1]

Image: *Lines: small group*, porcelain and brass. Photographer: Christina Liu

[1]Do Shop June 28, 2016

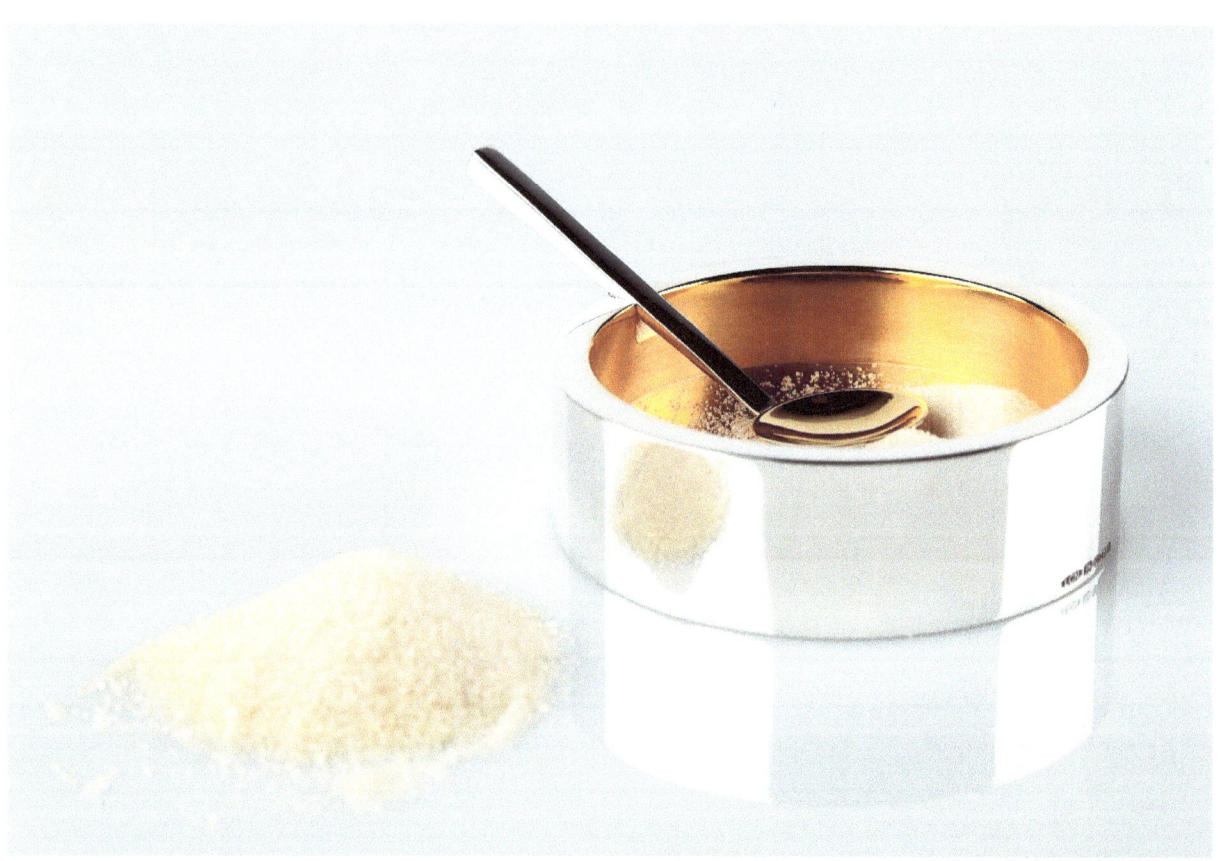

Loucinda Nims

2014 BA (Hons) 3D Contemporary Craft and Product, Bucks New University

Loucinda is a contemporary designer silversmith based in the West Berkshire countryside. After discovering her passion for making, Loucindas degree in 3D Contemporary Craft and Product enabled her to explore a variety of creative practices in ceramics, glass, metalwork and jewellery.

Her silverware work draws from a range of inspiration such as landscapes, preciousness and architecture. Exploring these themes, she creates a range of functional silverware and jewellery, which is both simple in shape and sensitive in design. Function is a significant part of her work, as she aims to make pieces which are beautiful to use, as well as look at.

Following graduation, Loucinda became resident at Bishopsland Educational Trust, the 'finishing school' for silversmiths and jewellers.

Image: *Sugar Bowl and Spoon*, sterling Silver and gold plate. Photography: Enrico Garofalo

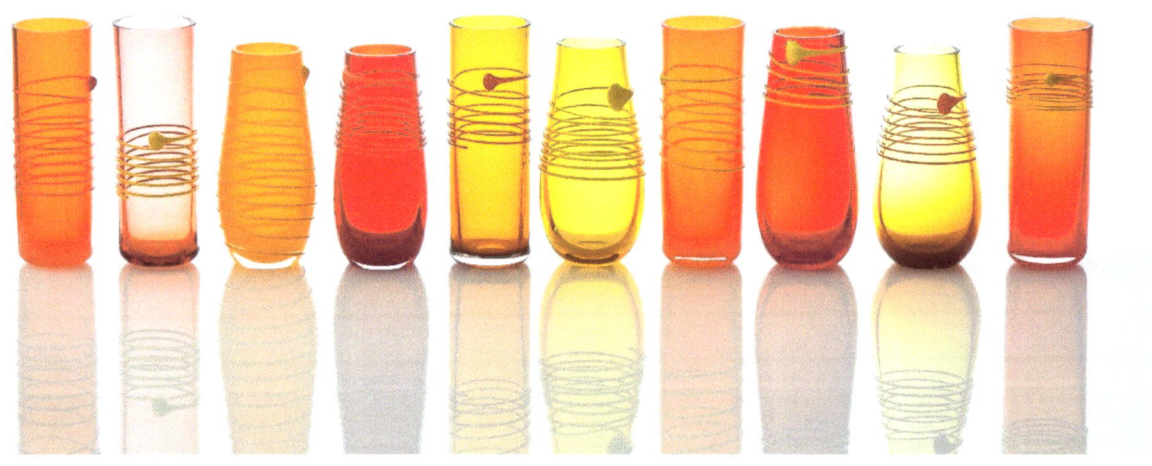

Catherine Bridget Phillips

2016 BA (Hons) Contemporary Craft and Products, Bucks New University

Catherine's work is handmade, using traditional and contemporary craft techniques. Working in both ceramic and glass, she creates designs inspired and informed by human interactions, often with hints of traditional aesthetics.

After almost a decade in the restaurant trade, Catherine designs tableware with the aim to enhance the pleasure of food and drink. With a focus on surface texture and pattern, her work is colourful and incredibly tactile.

Her range of stem-less prosecco glasses, created for a casual summer setting, take a modern spin on the traditional flute. The colours and shapes are inspired by pick 'n' mix sweet selections and add to the casual fun setting for which they are intended. Catherine received a 'Highly Commended' award for the glasses in the CGS Graduate Review 2016.

Image: *Pick n Mix Prosecco Glasses*, blown glass. Photography: Yeshen Venema

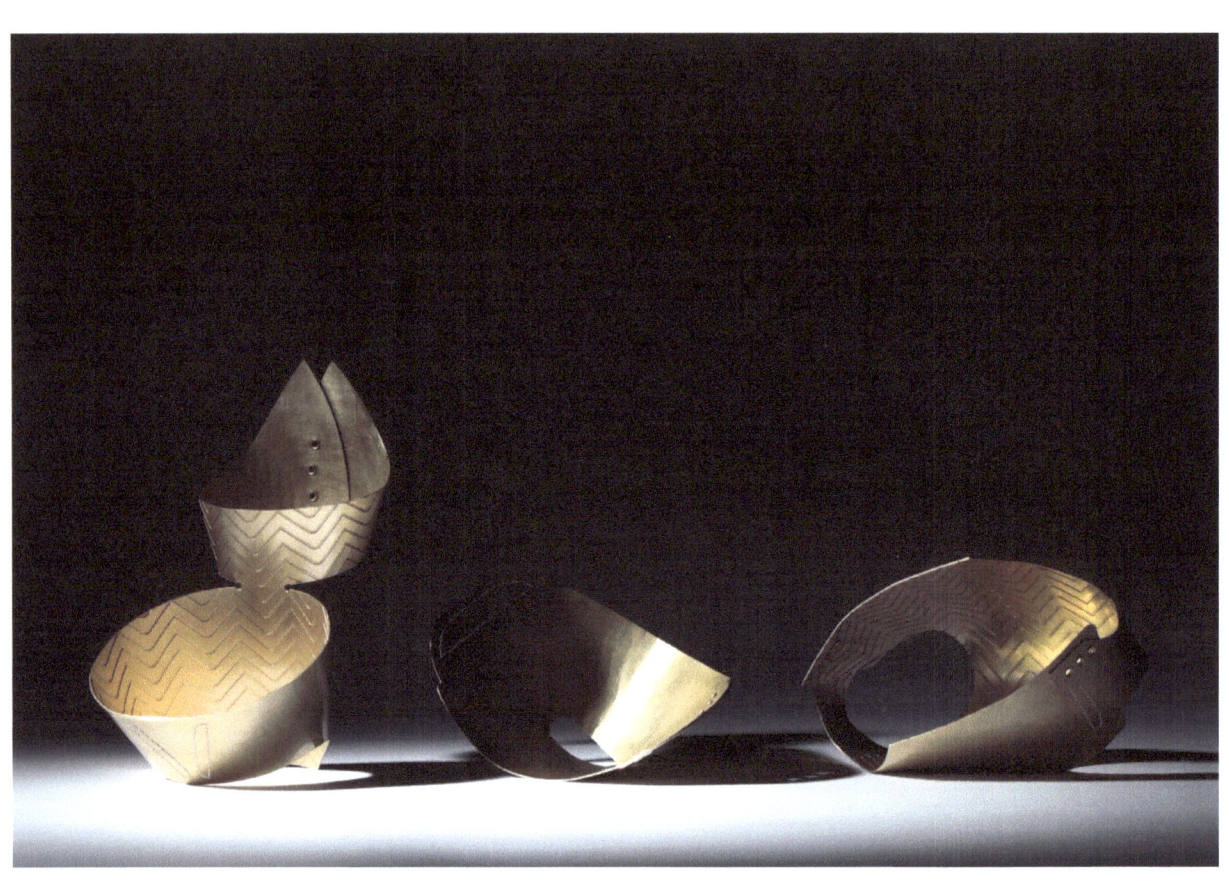

Suzanne Seed

2016 BA (Hons) Silversmithing, Goldsmithing and Jewellery, UCA, Rochester

Using a mixture of traditional and contemporary techniques, Suzanne's work consists of deconstructing, reconstructing and folding. She takes the starting point of a 3D product or form, and takes it back to its 2D roots to use these components as the foundation of her design. Using Adobe Illustrator and paper maquettes, she explores possibilities to create a new original design, often with no visual link to its origins. Suzanne adds a nod to the inspiration of the piece by using features of the original object as subtle design features in the finished piece.

Suzanne's designs have a minimalist feel with clean lines, and no additions for the sake of adornment. Her objects always start life as a flat sheet of metal and she relishes the experimentation of translating a 2D shape into a 3D resolved design. The mind designs, the hands construct and the metal dictates – the final outcome is a unity of the three.

One of Suzanne's designs, a silver golf ball marker, was shortlisted for the Make Your Mark Awards held by the London Assay office.

Image: *The Classic Collection*, etched Brass. Photography: Suzanne Seed

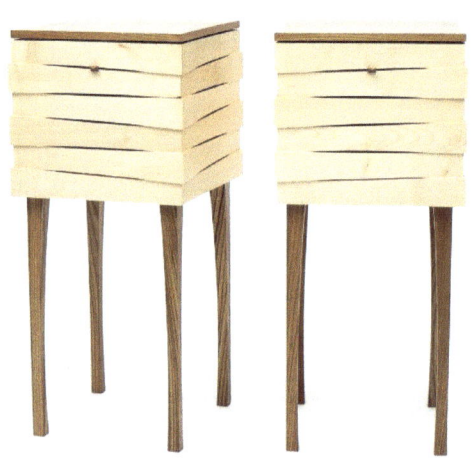

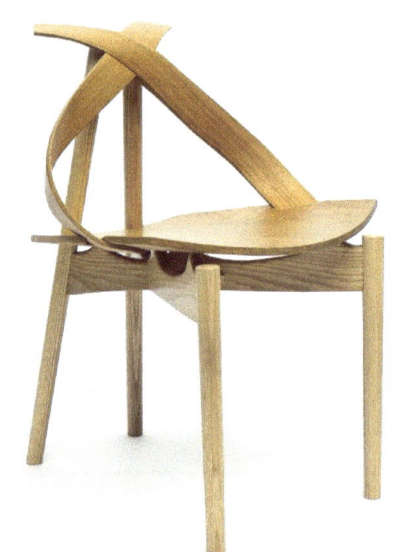

Troo Studio - Freya Whamond and Sam Bolt

2016 BA (Hons) Furniture: Design and Make, Rycotewood Furniture Centre, Oxford

2016 BA (Hons) Furniture: Design and Make, Rycotewood Furniture Centre, Oxford

Troo studio is a creative partnership that combines contemporary design with high quality craftsmanship. Freya and Sam trained at Rycotewood Furniture Centre, a part of the National School of Furniture in Oxford and together they design and make bespoke furniture and functional objects for the home.

They are greatly interested in material exploration and the making process. Working predominantly with timber, they experiment with traditional techniques, while pursuing a balance in design that celebrates the inherent beauty of this natural material through simplicity of form.

Freya and Sam believe in the importance of sensory interaction, not only as part of their practise but as part of the everyday. Their unique pieces are made to be explored by more than just the eye and are designed to invite a curious touch.

Image (left): Sam Bolt, *Reveal Cabinets* (Pair) sycamore and elm. Photography: Edward Fury
Image (right): Freya Whamond, *Laminated Chair*, oak and ash. Photography: Edward Fury

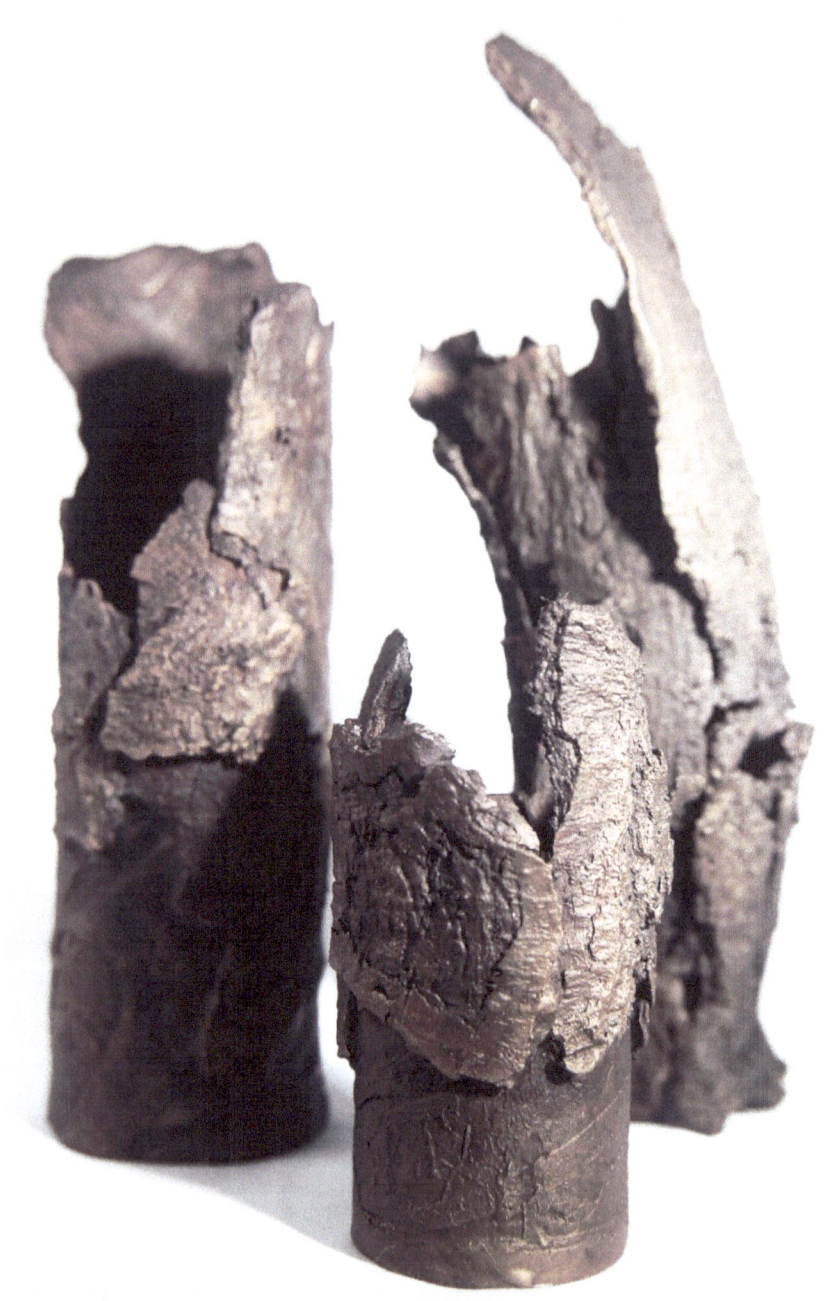

Rosie Wesley

2016 BA (Hons) Glass, Ceramics, Jewellery and Metalwork, UCA, Farnham

Working predominantly in non-precious metals, Rosie's range of sculptural work takes its inspiration from the New Forest, where she grew up. She is immeasurably interested in natural spaces of the forest; their sense of timelessness and human's instinctive connection to the materials found there. Her designs focus on three elements; texture, form and negative space. Each piece is a distinct response to a location within the New Forest; constructed from a combination of individual cast pieces of bark and materialised components based on negative spaces from the landscape, which are textured with markings based on her personal feelings and reactions to the environment. These elements come together to realise a subtle, instinctive form, embodying the essence of the landscape.

Rosie is interested in the concept of taking something from the landscape, transforming it and assembling it into something new; giving it a new life away from its original environment. The piece then no longer belongs to the original space, but stands for itself, and only carries the essence of the original space. With the occasional accompaniment of film, audio and photography, her work aims to create a calm and serene ambiance, encouraging the viewer to consider their personal place within natural environments and inspire them to experience these spaces more.

Image: *Ashurst I, II & III*, bronze with patina. Photography: Rosie Wesley